D1401139

WORLD COMMODITIES

Sugar

GARRY CHAPMAN » GARY HODGES

This edition first published in 2011 in the United States of America by Smart Apple Media.

Smart Apple Media
P.O. Box 3263
Mankato, MN, 56002

First published in 2010 by
MACMILLAN EDUCATION AUSTRALIA PTY LTD
15–19 Claremont Street, South Yarra 3141

Visit our web site at www.macmillan.com.au or go directly to www.macmillanlibrary.com.au

Associated companies and representatives throughout the world.

Copyright © Garry Chapman and Gary Hodges 2010

Library of Congress Cataloging-in-Publication Data

Chapman, Garry.
  Sugar / Garry Chapman and Gary Hodges.
    p. cm. — (World commodities)
  Includes index.
  ISBN 978-1-59920-587-8 (library binding)
  1. Sugar trade—Juvenile literature. 2. Sugar—Juvenile literature. 3. Sugar industry—Juvenile literature. I. Hodges, Gary. II. Title.
  HD9100.5.C47 2011
  338.4'76641—dc22
                        2010007309

Publisher: Carmel Heron   Designer: Ivan Finnegan (cover and text)
Commissioning Editor: Niki Horin   Page Layout: Ivan Finnegan
Managing Editor: Vanessa Lanaway   Photo Researcher: Lesya Bryndzia (management: Debbie Gallagher)
Editor: Laura Jeanne Gobal   Illustrators: Andy Craig and Nives Porcellato, 14, 15; Alan Laver, 17
Proofreader: Kirstie Innes-Will   Production Controller: Vanessa Johnson

Manufactured in the United States of America by Corporate Graphics, Minnesota.
052010

Acknowledgments
The author and the publisher are grateful to the following for permission to reproduce copyright material:

Front cover photograph of sugar cubes: 123RF/Matt Trommer

The Art Archive/Biblioteca Estense Modena/Alfredo Dagli Orti, **8** (right), /British Museum/Alfredo Dagli Orti, **8** (left), /Museum of London, **9** (bottom); Bloomberg via Getty Images/Keith Bedford, **19**, /Fridman, **24**; Corbis/ActionAid/Gideon Mendel, **21**, /Atlantide Phototravel, **7**, /Paulo Fridman, **28**, /Xinhua Press/Jon Fabrigar, **18**; Getty Images/AFP/Thony Belizaire, **26**, /AFP/Jacques Collet, **20**, /Dorling Kindersley, **4** (iron ore), /National Geographic/Winfield Parks, **22**; Gordon Ogletree, **29**; iStockphoto/ricardo azoury, **10** (middle right), /garysludden, **5**, /luminouslens, **13**; Photolibrary/The British Library, **9** (top), /Keith ErskineÂ, **12** (top right), /Monty Rakusen, **12** (bottom), /SPL/Robert Brook, **23**, /SPL/Maximilian Stock Ltd, **12** (left); Shutterstock/Alonbou, **6** (left), /Forest Badger, **4** (oil), /Hywit Dimyadi, **10** (middle left), /dusko, **11**, /IDAL, **4** (wheat), /Wen Mingming, **6** (right), /Alexander Raths, **25**, /Sapsiwai, **10** (bottom), /SVT Photography, **27**, /Don Tran, **10** (top), /Worldpics, **4** (coal), /yykkaa, **4** (sugar), /Magdalena Zurawska, **4** (coffee).

While every care has been taken to trace and acknowledge copyright, the publisher tenders their apologies for any accidental infringement where copyright has proved untraceable. Where the attempt has been unsuccessful, the publisher welcomes information that would redress the situation.

Please note: At the time of printing, the Internet addresses appearing in this book were correct. Owing to the dynamic nature of the Internet, however, we cannot guarantee that all of these addresses will remain correct.

This series is for my father, Ron Chapman, with gratitude. – Garry Chapman
This series is dedicated to the memory of Jean and Alex Ross, as well as my immediate family of Sue, Hannah and Jessica, my parents, Jim and Val, and my brother Leigh. – Gary Hodges

Contents

Glossary Words

When a word is printed in **bold**, you can look up its meaning in the Glossary on page 31.

What Is a World Commodity?

A commodity is any product for which someone is willing to pay money. A world commodity is a product that is traded across the world.

The World's Most Widely Traded Commodities

Many of the world's most widely traded commodities are **agricultural** products, such as coffee, sugar, and wheat, or **natural resources**, such as coal, iron ore, and oil. These commodities are produced in large amounts by people around the world.

Coal, coffee, iron ore, oil, sugar, and wheat are important commodities traded around the world.

Commodities and the World's Economy

Whenever the world's **demand** for a commodity increases or decreases, the price of this commodity goes up or down by the same amount everywhere. Prices usually vary from day to day. The daily trade in world commodities plays a key role in the state of the world's **economy**.

MORE ABOUT...
The Quality of Commodities

When people, businesses, or countries buy a commodity, they assume that its quality will be consistent. Oil is an example of a commodity. When people trade in oil, all barrels of oil are considered to be of the same quality regardless of where they come from.

Sugar Is a Commodity

Sugar is a crystalline substance, used by people all over the world to sweeten the taste of food and drinks. It is also used in the manufacture of fruit juices, syrups, cakes, and candy.

A Natural Sweetener

Sugar can take several forms, including sucrose, fructose, and lactose. Sucrose is the most commonly used form of sugar and is sometimes called table sugar. It occurs naturally in fruits, vegetables, and honey, but can be produced in commercial amounts only from sugar cane or sugar beet. When we refer to sugar in this book, we are referring to sucrose.

Sugar is a **carbohydrate**. It provides the human body with energy and contains no **additives** or **preservatives**.

Worldwide Demand

Sugar is in demand all over the world. About 70 percent of all sugar produced is used in its country of origin. The rest is **exported,** either to countries unable to grow sugar-producing crops or unable to produce enough to meet their own needs. More than 100 countries produce sugar commercially.

One of the most popular uses of sugar is to sweeten drinks, such as tea and coffee.

Where Is Sugar Grown and Where Is It Consumed?

Two very different types of plant—sugar cane and sugar beet—provide the world with most of its sugar. These plants grow in very different climates. Their product is consumed all over the world.

Sugar Cane

Sugar cane is a tall grass with jointed stalks that grow several feet tall. Its stalks contain sugar. Sugar cane is grown in **tropical** and subtropical regions, where it is moist, warm, and sunny.

Sugar Beet

Sugar beet is a root vegetable belonging to the beetroot family. It has a leafy stem and a large root. Sugar is found in its root. Sugar beet is mainly grown in places with a cool, **temperate** climate, such as parts of Europe, Japan, and the United States.

Sugar comes from two main sources: sugar cane (left) and sugar beet (right).

COMMODITY FACT!

More than 100 countries produce sugar. About 78 percent of that sugar comes from sugar cane. The rest comes from sugar beet.

Sugar Production and Consumption

Brazil is the world's largest producer of sugar cane. In Brazil, sugar cane is grown as a food product and also as a source of ethanol—an environmentally friendly **biofuel** for vehicles. Most cars in Brazil run on a mix of regular gasoline and ethanol.

India is the world's largest consumer of sugar. More than 60 percent of the sugar in the country is consumed by food-processing companies and the rest by the public.

Barbados, in the Caribbean, is a country with a thriving sugar-cane industry.

THE WORLD'S MAJOR PRODUCERS AND CONSUMERS OF SUGAR (2008)

Producer	Amount of Sugar Produced	Consumer	Amount of Sugar Consumed
Brazil	35.52 million tons (32.29 million t)	India	24.81 million tons (22.55 million t)
India	28.53 million tons (25.94 million t)	European Union	22.52 million tons (20.47 million t)
European Union	18.02 million tons (16.38 million t)	China	16.20 million tons (14.73 million t)
China	16.94 million tons (15.40 million t)	Brazil	13.05 million tons (11.86 million t)
Thailand	8.55 million tons (7.77 million t)	United States	10.80 million tons (9.81 million t)

Timeline: **The History of Sugar**

Humans have enjoyed the sweet taste of sugar for more than 5,000 years. The Indians were the first to determine how to turn sugar cane juice into crystals. Today, people all over the world enjoy sugar.

3000 B.C.
In India, people chew raw sugar cane for its sweet taste. They learn to crush the stalks to extract the juice.

about 650
The Persians discover how to mold brown sugar into cone-shaped loaves. Sugar loaves become the most efficient way to transport and trade sugar for the next thousand years.

1099
Soldiers bring sugar home to England from the Crusades in the Middle East. European **importers** establish a sugar trade with Arab merchants. Sugar is a luxury item available only to the wealthy.

3000 B.C.

A.D. 550
Indian sugar-makers teach the Chinese and Persians how to grow sugar cane and produce sugar.

about 750
Arab invaders conquer Persia and learn about growing sugar cane. They establish the first sugar-cane plantations, mills, and **refineries**, and they trade sugar with lands bordering the Mediterranean Sea.

1493
The explorer Christopher Columbus brings sugar-cane plants to the Caribbean.

This sculpture, dating back to 650 B.C., shows people growing sugar cane.

400
Indians begin to make sugar syrup, which is cooled to make crystals. Cakes of dried crystals are traded with other parts of Asia, such as China and Persia (modern-day Iran).

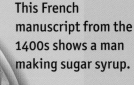

This French manuscript from the 1400s shows a man making sugar syrup.

8

1500s

The Dutch, Portuguese, and Spanish bring sugar cane to their **colonies** in South America and the Caribbean. African slaves provide labor for the plantations. Sugar is shipped back to refineries in Europe.

1747

Sugar beet is identified as a source of sugar. It allows Europeans to produce sugar in the temperate climate of Europe.

This painting from 1823 shows slaves cutting sugar cane in Antigua, in the Caribbean.

1770s

The Industrial Revolution, a period of time when manufacturing by machines in factories grew in importance and scale, introduces more efficient steam-driven machinery to the processing of sugar.

1920s

Sugar-cane based ethanol fuel is first used in Brazil, following the introduction of the automobile.

1979

The Fiat 147, built in Brazil, becomes the first modern car capable of running only on ethanol.

A.D. 2010

1700s

The sugar trade becomes very valuable to European countries with colonies in South America and the Caribbean. The Caribbean becomes the world's largest producer of sugar.

1880

Sugar beet replaces sugar cane as the main source of sugar in Europe.

2010

Sugar is used extensively in food preparation, but people are encouraged to use it in moderation. This is because eating too much sugar can lead to health problems.

The sugar loaf and mold pictured here are from the 1500s. They were found in London, England.

9

How Is Sugar Made?

Sugar is made from sugar cane and sugar beet. Both plants produce sugar in large amounts for harvesting and processing.

Sugar Cane

Sugar cane is a tall grass which contains sugar in its stalks. Once planted, it takes about 9 to 16 months to grow. It is usually harvested between June and December.

Planting Cuttings

Sugar cane grows from cuttings planted by hand. It reaches full growth in about a year. Although new stalks will grow after each harvest, each cycle will offer a little less sugar than the previous one. After about ten cycles, a new cutting must be planted.

Harvesting by Hand

In some **developing countries**, the cane is cut by hand, using large knives. Before harvesting the cane, the fields may be burned to rid them of unwanted leaves and dangerous snakes, leaving the stalks and roots unharmed.

Harvesting by Machine

In other countries, the rotating, sharp blades of a combine harvester cut the stalks at the base, leaving the roots untouched. The leaves are stripped and blown back into the cane field, while the stalks are placed in a large wagon.

COMMODITY FACT!

Sugar cane is usually grown in large plantations, or cane fields, where it sometimes yields up to 44 pounds (20 kg) of sugar for every 11 square feet (1 square m) of land.

Transporting to the Mill

It is important to transport the cane quickly to a sugar mill nearby before it loses its sugar content. The cane is often moved by train or truck.

Sugar Beet

Sugar beet is a vegetable that stores sugar in its large, bulb-shaped root. It is mostly grown in the Northern Hemisphere, where it is planted in the spring (late March and early April) and harvested in the fall (late September and October).

This modern vehicle is used to harvest sugar beet quickly and easily.

Sowing and Harvesting

Traditionally, sugar beet was sown and harvested by hand. During the harvest, one person would pull the beet from the ground by its leaves and another would slice the top of the root and the leaves off with a sharp tool. The beets were then loaded into carts and sent for processing.

Today, sugar beet is sown and harvested by machine. A roto beater removes the leaves and the top of the root before a harvester lifts the root, cleans away the soil, and places it into a truck. The truck then transports the beets for processing.

Preparing Sugar for Consumption

Once harvested, sugar cane and sugar beet are processed in similar ways to extract sugar.

Processing Sugar Cane

When sugar cane reaches the sugar mill, the entire stalk is processed to extract sugar, and the leftover material is saved for different uses.

Washing, Chopping, and Crushing

First, the cane is washed and chopped into small pieces. Then it is shredded by revolving blades. Water is added and the shredded cane is crushed by large rollers. This process releases cane juice, which contains about 10 to 15 percent sugar.

Filtering

The cane juice is filtered, then mixed with **calcium hydroxide** and allowed to sit. The calcium hydroxide catches impurities and settles them for easy removal. The cane juice is then boiled to **evaporate** much of the liquid. This creates a syrup containing about 60 percent pure sugar.

Crystallization

The syrup is sprinkled with sugar crystals to produce a mixture of clear crystals and sticky, brown **molasses**. The mixture is then spun rapidly to separate the crystals from the molasses. The crystals are cleaned with steam and air-dried. As the sugar cools, more crystals form. The raw brown sugar is stored, ready to be sent to a refinery.

Processing Sugar Beet

Sugar beet is washed, sliced, and soaked in hot water to extract the sugar. Impurities are removed, and the liquid is filtered, then heated to evaporate much of the water. The remaining sticky syrup, known as molasses, contains more than 60 percent pure sugar. Once cool, the syrup is spun rapidly to separate sugar crystals from the molasses. The crystals are cleaned with steam and air-dried.

Refining Sugar

By the time it reaches a refinery, there is no difference between sugar produced from sugar cane and that produced from sugar beet. At the refinery, raw sugar is purified to produce pure-white sugar. This often requires treatment with chemicals and additional filtration, crystallization, and spinning. The sugar crystals are then sifted to produce different types of sugar.

There are many different types of sugar, each suited to different uses.

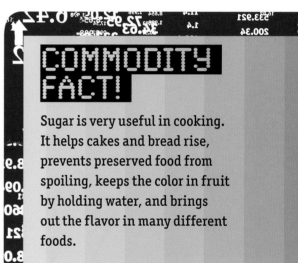

COMMODITY FACT!

Sugar is very useful in cooking. It helps cakes and bread rise, prevents preserved food from spoiling, keeps the color in fruit by holding water, and brings out the flavor in many different foods.

DIFFERENT TYPES OF SUGAR

Name	Appearance	Uses
Granulated sugar	Pure-white crystals	Household uses • sweetening drinks
Sanding sugar	Larger, coarser grains	Decorating cakes and cookies
Superfine sugar	Smaller, finer grains	Baking
Powdered sugar	Very fine grains	Icing cakes
Brown sugar	Brown grains, often sticky	Household uses • sweetening drinks • enhancing the flavor of food

The Sugar Trade

The sugar trade is one of the most complex trades in the world. It involves subsidies, quotas, price controls, and preferential arrangements.

Protecting Domestic Sugar Growers

Many governments try to protect their **domestic** sugar growers so that these growers are able to make a decent living from growing sugar crops. This is usually achieved through subsidies or quotas. A subsidy is an amount of money paid by the government to a grower to lower the cost of farming sugar crops. A quota places limits on the amount of the product that can be imported. With fewer imports entering the country, there is less competition, making it easier for domestic growers to sell their products.

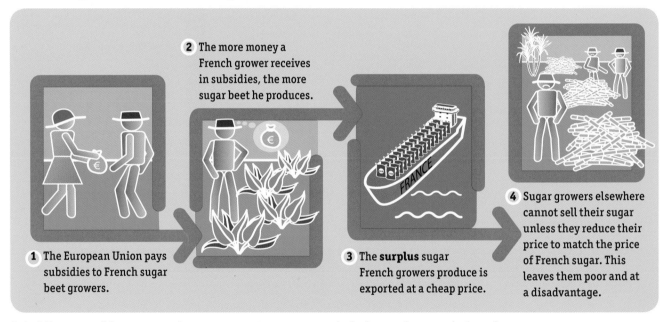

1 The European Union pays subsidies to French sugar beet growers.

2 The more money a French grower receives in subsidies, the more sugar beet he produces.

3 The **surplus** sugar French growers produce is exported at a cheap price.

4 Sugar growers elsewhere cannot sell their sugar unless they reduce their price to match the price of French sugar. This leaves them poor and at a disadvantage.

Subsidies are paid to growers by governments to protect their domestic sugar industries.

Selling Surplus Sugar

Once their domestic sugar needs have been met, some countries try to sell their surplus sugar to other countries. Usually, this means their surplus sugar is "dumped" on the world market at a heavily reduced price so that it will sell easily. Unfortunately, the cheap surplus sugar brings the world price down, making it very difficult for growers from developing countries to get a reasonable price for their sugar.

Exchanges

An exchange is a place where commodities, such as sugar, are bought and sold. At an exchange, sugar is bought and sold in both the futures market and spot market.

The Futures Market

Trading in the futures market involves buying and selling contracts that are set in the future. Buyers and sellers agree on a price, which will be paid when the sugar is delivered at a date in the future.

The futures trading of sugar takes place in three main stages. The sugar buyer is agreeing to buy sugar at a future date for a set price.

2 Some time later, a severe frost ruins sugar beet crops in France and pushes the world price of sugar up to US$735 per ton (0.9 t).

1 A sugar buyer in Germany and a seller in France agree on a price of US$730 per ton (0.9 t) of sugar to be delivered on a set date.

3 On the agreed date, the sugar is sent to the buyer. The buyer has benefited because he bought the sugar at less than the world price.

2 Cash is exchanged electronically from the buyer to the seller.

3 The sugar cane is immediately sent to the ethanol factory.

1 An ethanol producer in Brazil buys sugar cane from a domestic plantation.

The spot trading of sugar is a simple transaction between a sugar grower and an ethanol producer that takes place in three main stages.

The Spot Market

In the spot market, buyers and sellers agree on a price for the immediate exchange of goods. This means sugar is delivered to the buyer as soon as it is purchased.

Supply and Demand

The sugar trade is determined by **supply** and demand. When consumers are eager to buy the commodity, the demand for sugar increases. Consumers rely on producers to supply it.

Factors Affecting Supply

It is difficult to make a good living from selling sugar crops. The cost of harvesting equipment, fertilizers, and labor can be very high. This is why some countries pay subsidies to domestic sugar-growers. Subsidies ensure that sugar-growers can continue supplying the market. Supply may also be affected by natural events, such as droughts or floods, which can destroy crops. This would affect domestic and export supplies as well as cause prices to rise.

Factors Affecting Demand

The demand for sugar is usually quite high because it is used in the preparation of food and drinks all over the world. As the world moves toward the use of alternative clean fuels in vehicles, the growing preference for ethanol, a biofuel, may also boost demand for sugar.

THE WORLD'S TOP EXPORTERS AND IMPORTERS OF SUGAR (2008)

Exporter	Amount of Sugar Exported	Importer	Amount of Sugar Imported
Brazil	22.15 million tons (20.14 million t)	Russia	2.77 million tons (2.52 million t)
Thailand	5.62 million tons (5.11 million t)	United States	2.61 million tons (2.37 million t)
India	4.65 million tons (4.23 million t)	European Union	2.21 million tons (2.01 million t)
Australia	3.62 million tons (3.29 million t)	Nigeria	1.73 million tons (1.57 million t)
Guatemala	1.46 million tons (1.33 million t)	Iran	1.60 million tons (1.45 million t)

Price Variations

When the global demand for sugar is greater than its supply, the price of sugar increases. In the same way, when the supply of sugar is greater than the demand for it, the world sugar price falls.

THE RISE AND FALL OF THE WORLD PRICE OF SUGAR

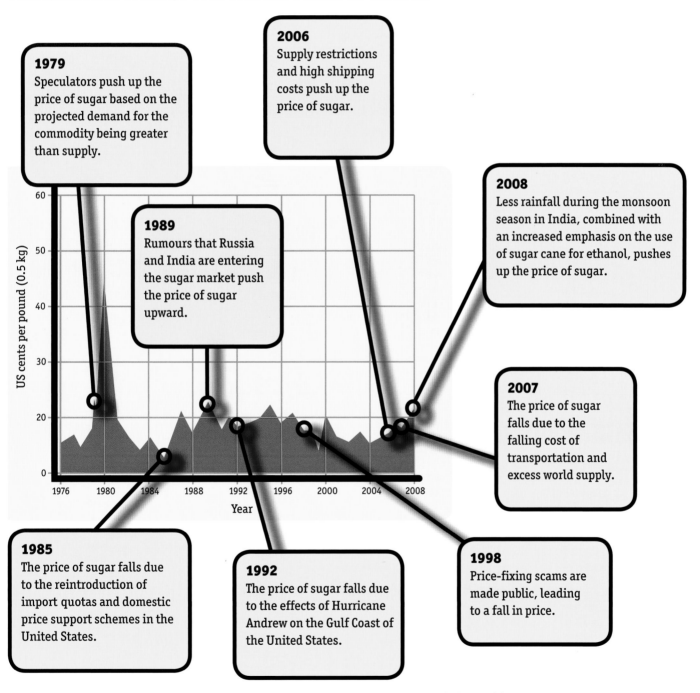

1979
Speculators push up the price of sugar based on the projected demand for the commodity being greater than supply.

2006
Supply restrictions and high shipping costs push up the price of sugar.

2008
Less rainfall during the monsoon season in India, combined with an increased emphasis on the use of sugar cane for ethanol, pushes up the price of sugar.

1989
Rumours that Russia and India are entering the sugar market push the price of sugar upward.

2007
The price of sugar falls due to the falling cost of transportation and excess world supply.

1985
The price of sugar falls due to the reintroduction of import quotas and domestic price support schemes in the United States.

1992
The price of sugar falls due to the effects of Hurricane Andrew on the Gulf Coast of the United States.

1998
Price-fixing scams are made public, leading to a fall in price.

The world price of sugar experiences highs and lows over time. Events around the world influence the supply of and demand for the commodity, which changes the price.

Codes of Practice

Codes of practice govern the way most commodities are traded internationally. The purpose of these codes is to ensure that commodities are fairly priced and traded.

International Regulation

The sugar trade is regulated by the World Trade Organization (WTO). It is an international body with more than 150 member countries. The WTO helps countries negotiate trade agreements, which will ensure that any business between them is conducted fairly. Disputes over trade issues may be dealt with by the WTO. However, it is the governments which signed the agreements that are ultimately responsible for settling disputes.

In January 2010, protesters gathered outside the office of the Department of Trade and Industry in Manila, the Philippines, to demand the regulation of sugar and bread prices.

The Anti-Dumping Agreement

Perhaps the most important agreement governing the sugar trade is the Anti-Dumping Agreement. It aims to prevent large sugar producers, such as the United States and the European Union, from dumping their surplus sugar on the world market. Both the United States and the European Union use subsidies and quotas to protect their sugar producers. Under such systems, growers often produce much more sugar than their domestic markets need. The excess is dumped on the world market at low prices. This forces the world price down. It means smaller producers earn less for their sugar.

International Sugar Organization

The International Sugar Organization (ISO) is based in London and made up of 85 member countries. It was set up to administer the International Sugar Agreement of 1992. Although not strictly a regulatory body, the ISO aims to improve international cooperation on sugar-related issues. It also sponsors projects that help developing countries to make their agricultural practices more efficient.

MORE ABOUT...

The International Sugar Agreement (1992)

In March 1992, ISO members established an International Sugar Agreement. It aimed to improve cooperation between sugar-trading countries, provide governments with a forum in which to discuss sugar-related issues, and provide information about sugar trading. The United States was not prepared to consent to certain aspects of the agreement and soon quit the ISO.

The ISO aims to improve working conditions in developing countries.

19

International Politics and Sugar

Several key issues dominate the way the world sugar trade operates. Subsidies and quotas are two such issues. These practices can affect the price of sugar and can also limit the profits other countries make from selling their sugar.

United States

The sugar **lobby** in the United States is very powerful. Lobbying has resulted in various sugar-related initiatives being made into law. The *Farm Security and Rural Investment Act* of 2002 guarantees sugar growers an attractive price for their sugar, supported by tough quotas and taxes on imports. The domestic price of sugar has generally been around three times the value of the international price of sugar, as a result of protective measures.

European Union

Similar pressures are placed on political parties, candidates, and elected representatives in the European Union. The Common Agricultural Policy was created to favor growers in the European Union over those in other countries. However, the policy is slowly being revised to lower quotas and change the way subsidies are handed out, so that surpluses are reduced.

A person dressed as the grim reaper stands on a pile of sugar beets as part of a protest against the European Union's plan to cut subsidies in 2005.

Developing Countries

Developing countries have few options for dealing with sugar prices that have been lowered by cheap surpluses entering the market. One strategy that may help these countries in such a situation is to approach the World Trade Organization (WTO) for assistance. They could also lobby **developed countries** for preferential status in the sugar trade, which is what the European Union awarded to African, Caribbean, and Pacific countries as part of its Common Agricultural Policy.

"Low world sugar prices and the dumping of sugar are a problem ... I would like to see sugar subsidies cut and a global levelling of the playing field. European farmers should farm something more suitable to their climate. This would allow developing countries, particularly the small-scale growers, to grow more sugar cane for the world market, which would improve my situation. I can't grow anything other than sugar cane."

Mzo Mzoneli, sugar cane grower, Natal, South Africa
(Source: www.maketradefair.com/en/index.php?file=sugar_casestudy01.htm)

These sugar growers in Kenya, East Africa, are hoeing their land to plant tomatoes instead of sugar, because the local sugar factory went out of business.

Environmental Issues and Sugar

Much of the environmental damage caused by sugar production occurred many years ago, when the industry was new. Though production equipment and farming practices have changed over time to lessen the damage, some practices are still in use today and cause concern.

Air Pollution

For many years, growers burned their cane fields before the harvest to rid them of snakes and unwanted leaves. This practice still occurs in some countries, especially those with poor access to modern harvesting machinery. The burning of cane fields releases great amounts of polluting gases into the atmosphere. This contributes to **global warming** and **climate change**.

Destruction of the Landscape

In the early years of sugar-cane farming, many acres of natural forest were cleared to make way for cane plantations. Many plant and animal **habitats** and species were lost to this process. Some of these regions have never recovered. Today, many governments have strict rules regarding the use of land for farming.

This rain forest region in Queensland, Australia, has been cleared to grow sugar cane. The only trees that remain are growing on the ridges.

Problems with Waterways

When forests are cleared to make way for cane plantations, **soil erosion** results. Soil and fertilizers often get washed or blown into rivers, streams, and other waterways. They pollute the water and change the **ecosystems** of plants and animals that depend on these waterways.

During processing, water is used to wash the cane, to make the syrup, and to clean equipment. Wastewater from these processes contains harmful substances that can contaminate waterways if disposed of inappropriately. Most sugar-processing plants now have wastewater treatment systems that remove the harmful substances.

Processing sugar cane produces a lot of wastewater, which can pollute the surrounding environment if it is not treated before disposal.

MORE ABOUT...
Soil Erosion

Sugar cane can be grown on steep hillsides, but this leads to high rates of soil erosion. In the Caribbean and South Africa, sugar cane is sometimes grown on hillsides that are more than twice as steep as the recommended slope of eight percent.

Social Issues and Sugar

Sugar cane is often grown in developing countries, where the biggest social issues are the pay and working conditions of sugar growers. Sugar also plays a part in public health issues, such as tooth decay and obesity.

Protecting the Welfare of Sugar Growers

Sugar growers in developing countries are usually poor and make very little from the sale of their sugar crops, due to conditions in the world market. They may also be taken advantage of by the companies that buy their sugar crops for processing. To protect them, governments can introduce strict guidelines for the domestic trade of sugar. Governments can also introduce subsidies or other forms of financial assistance.

Brazilian sugar cane is used in the production of ethanol, or álcool, for vehicles. This increases the income of Brazil's sugar growers.

Brazil

Brazil, the world's largest sugar producer, found a way to boost the welfare of sugar growers by introducing a biofuel program in the 1970s. About half of the sugar cane grown in the country is now used to produce ethanol. The ethanol industry supports sugar growers by maintaining schools and providing access to healthcare services for their families. Money from the ethanol industry also helps provide a decent wage for sugar growers.

Sugar and Public Health

Sugar is often associated with public health issues. Consuming too many sugary foods and drinks may cause a number of diseases and health conditions.

Tooth Decay

Sugar can lead to tooth decay. Bacteria in our mouths convert sugar to lactic acid, which eats away at our teeth. To prevent this, brushing and flossing after every meal are recommended, especially if the meal has a high sugar content.

Obesity

Eating a lot of sugary and fatty foods is a direct cause of obesity. People who are obese have a greater risk of developing diabetes, a disease that prevents the body from correctly processing sugar.

Enjoy Sugar in Moderation

The sugar industry promotes the importance of sugar for a healthy lifestyle. It recommends a balanced diet and regular exercise as the ideal way to maintain good health. It also recommends that sugar be consumed in moderation.

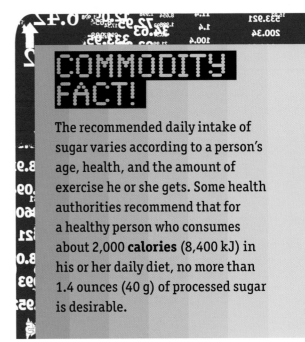

COMMODITY FACT!

The recommended daily intake of sugar varies according to a person's age, health, and the amount of exercise he or she gets. Some health authorities recommend that for a healthy person who consumes about 2,000 **calories** (8,400 kJ) in his or her daily diet, no more than 1.4 ounces (40 g) of processed sugar is desirable.

Cookies and cakes contain a lot of sugar, which can create health problems.

Is the Sugar Industry Sustainable?

To sustain something is to keep it going for a very long time. There are three aspects to keeping the sugar industry sustainable: making sure sugar-growing communities can survive, protecting the environment in which sugar is grown, and maintaining the demand for sugar.

Caring for Communities

The communities that rely on jobs in the sugar industry must remain sustainable. This means growers must make enough money from their sugar crops to support themselves and their families. To achieve this, prices must be kept at competitive levels for all, and trade should be made fairer. Governments can also do more to help their disadvantaged sugar growers. Brazil, the world's largest producer of sugar, has taken steps to ensure the sustainability of its sugar growers by developing its ethanol industry. In the ethanol industry, growers have an additional buyer for their sugar crops, which means a more stable source of income.

In developing countries, such as Haiti, in the Caribbean, sugar growers struggle to make a living from selling sugar.

Protecting the Environment

A number of changes to the way sugar cane is grown and harvested have improved the environmental sustainability of the industry. Harvesting machines have reduced the need for fields to be burned. Improved fertilizers mean the soil and waterways are better looked after. Major cane-producing countries, including Australia and the United States, now have guidelines to ensure environmental sustainability in the sugar industry. These guidelines include finding other uses for the waste products from sugar processing and ensuring that wastewater is properly treated before it enters surrounding waterways.

Ongoing Demand for Sugar

The demand for sugar is likely to always exist because the commodity is widely used in drinks and food. The demand for sugar crops is expected to grow as the biofuels industry develops. In recent years, people have learned that in order to protect Earth from global warming, cleaner alternative fuels must be used by industries, vehicles, and homes. Ethanol is one solution to the problem. It is already widely used in Brazil, and one day, it might be used in more countries around the world. To meet a growing demand for ethanol, more sugar cane may also be required.

Burning cane fields contributes to global warming.

COMMODITY FACT!

The United States and Brazil lead the world in ethanol production. Together they produce about 90 percent of all ethanol.

The Future of the Sugar Industry

The sugar industry faces an interesting future. Ensuring that sugar growers are paid fairly for their crops, people's changing diets, and innovations in technology will have an impact on the industry and the importance of sugar as a commodity in the future.

Will the Sugar Trade Change?

The United States and the European Union provide subsidies that protect their sugar industries and limit competition from other countries. The surplus sugar they dump on the world market lowers the world price of sugar. Struggling sugar growers in developing countries will continue to earn very little, unless they also begin to receive government assistance or find alternative sources of income.

More ethanol factories may be built to meet the expected growth in demand for biofuels.

The Rise of the Ethanol Industry

The use of ethanol as a transportation fuel may grow in the future, especially as a substitute for gasoline. Brazil, which is one of the leaders of the ethanol industry, has offered to increase its ethanol exports to India and has announced plans to provide biofuel research and production facilities for Africa. It is eager to establish a world market for biofuels, such as sugar-based ethanol. However, as more land is set aside for sugar-cane plantations rather than food crops, food prices may start to rise.

Switching to Sugar Substitutes

Medical studies suggest that there is a link between excessive sugar consumption and health conditions, such as obesity, tooth decay, and diabetes. Many health-conscious people have started choosing foods with low sugar content or using sugar substitutes.

Improved Farming Practices

Now that there is better understanding about the impact of sugar-cane farming on water quality and global warming, farming methods have changed. Cane growers now mulch their fields with waste cane products. This solves a waste disposal problem, improves the quality of the soil, and helps prevent soil erosion. A process called drip fertigation has lessened the harm caused by chemical fertilizers. Using drip fertigation, fertilizers are drip fed to the plants with pinpoint accuracy.

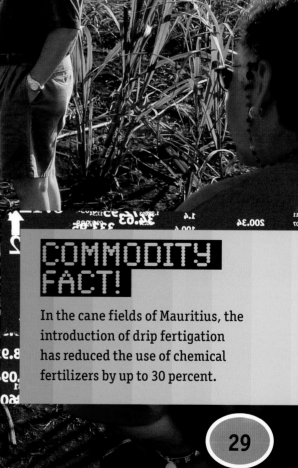

In the future, more efficient farming practices, such as drip fertigation, may help to make sugar cane a more sustainable crop.

COMMODITY FACT!

In the cane fields of Mauritius, the introduction of drip fertigation has reduced the use of chemical fertilizers by up to 30 percent.

Find Out More

Web Sites for Further Information

- ### All about sugar cane
  Learn more about sugar cane and how it is grown.
  www.plantcultures.org/plants/sugar_cane_landing.html

- ### An introduction to sugar beet
  Learn more about how sugar beet is grown in the United Kingdom.
  www.ukagriculture.com/crops/sugar_beet_farming.cfm

- ### Types of sugar
  Learn more about the different types of sugar and how they are used.
  www.food-info.net/uk/products/sugar/types.htm

- ### Sugar and your health
  Learn more about the health advantages and disadvantages of sugary foods.
  www.betterhealth.vic.gov.au/bhcv2/bhcarticles.nsf/pages/Sugar

Focus Questions

These questions might help you think about some of the issues raised in this book.

- What are some of the practices that have been introduced in recent times to ensure that the production of sugar does not harm the environment?

- What are the benefits and disadvantages of the United States and the European Union providing subsidies to protect domestic sugar growers?

- Do government subsidies and quotas harm or help the sugar industry?

- Should ethanol be the fuel of choice for all motorists?

Glossary

additives	substances added to food so it tastes or looks better
agricultural	related to farming or used for farming
biofuel	a fuel which is made from living things or their waste
calcium hydroxide	a white powder used to make cement, plaster, and other products
calories	units of measurement for energy
carbohydrate	one of a group of foods that are broken down by the body to produce energy
climate change	a change in the world's weather conditions over a period of time due to natural events or human activities
colonies	countries which have been settled and are governed by a more powerful country
demand	the amount of a product consumers want to buy
developed countries	countries that are very industrialized
developing countries	countries in the early stages of becoming industrialized
domestic	relating to a person's own country
economy	a system that organizes the production, distribution, and exchange of goods and services, as well as incomes
ecosystems	communities of plants and animals that interact with one another and with the environments in which they live
European Union	an association of 27 European countries set up in 1993, with its own currency and market
evaporate	change from a liquid to a gas, especially by heating
exported	sold or sent to another country
global warming	the gradual increase in world temperatures over time
habitats	the natural environments of plants or animals
importers	people, companies, or countries which buy or bring in a product from another country
lobby	a group of people who try to influence lawmakers or other public officials on behalf of a particular cause
molasses	a sticky, brown syrup made from sugar plants
mulch	loose materials, such as woodchips or straw, spread over the ground to protect the soil and hold in moisture
natural resources	the naturally occurring, useful wealth of a region or country, such as land, forests, coal, oil, gas, and water
preservatives	chemicals used to preserve food
refineries	factories where raw sugar is processed to create different sugar products
soil erosion	the loss of soil caused by wind blowing it away or water flowing over the soil and washing it away
supply	the amount of a product that producers are able to sell
surplus	an amount which is more than is needed
temperate	not very hot and not very cold
tropical	hot, wet, and humid

Index